F+AIL

INTO SUCCESS

A+

MICHAEL L. GAINES Ed.D.

Publisher: Created Solutions LLC

Copyright © 2014 Michael L. Gaines. . All rights reserved worldwide.

ISBN 9780692828991

Acknowledgments

To Jill, Alison, Amia, Alexia, John, and Mitchell. Thank you for being great teachers. It is my prayer that you all learn the power of "Failing into Success."

Mrs. Jonella D. Gaines my mother and my constant friend: thank you for being my earliest cheerleader and supporter. Thank you to my siblings (Gaines & Baker Clans) all of you have added to me and have helped me to grow through my failure.

We all stand on the shoulders of someone and often there is a significant individual who prompts you to take steps along your journey. My father Charles T. Gaines Jr. is a man who stood head and shoulders above many. His commitment to education and advancing his family is a debt I can never repay. Mr. Jerry Gore is a giant whose legacy lives on in the pages of this book. His prompting to "write my story" gave me the courage to stay the course. Thanks to these two men who I pray to see again one day.

Table of Contents

5

Chapter 1: The Failure/Success Paradox

I have been fortunate to have been able to see the shiny side of success and the rusty side of failure often in my short life. Through all of my experiences of life, I have come to believe that failure is not as bad as I once imagined it to be.

This journey called life is interestingly funny in that it is like a glacier: It is persistent, steady and powerful, with the ability to split or steamroll anything which dares to come into contact with it. Although you may not see glaciers moving, they are in constant friction, change, and motion. I believe life shares these attributes as well. Have you noticed that life will not leave you alone and just let you be? It has a way of staying in your face.

We have all heard the sayings, "Life happens" or "Life comes at you fast." Often said with tongue-in-cheek, I believe these thoughts capture a very important principle. Life waits for no one, coddles no one, and favors no one.

Life as we know it is made up of many moving parts. The challenge is to make it through the gauntlet of life without getting completely incapacitated by the ebbs and flows and in-and-outs of life. How do we navigate this complex maze without being worn out by the tenacious and persistent challenges that life throws at us? I believe that understanding the Failure/Success Paradox will help. What is this paradox of life?

" Without failure, there is no success."

There are those who run from failure and try to avoid it at all costs. I must admit I spent a large portion of my life running from failure, or at the very least covering and hiding my failures from as many people as possible. I learned very quickly that I could not cover up my failures fast enough before they were discovered by someone else. I also discovered that failures cannot be covered, they must be carried. However, the more I tried to hide my failures, the more difficult it became to carry them.

Since I had always viewed failure as something to be avoided, I was sure that my failure somehow revealed a flaw in me. On one hand maybe, that is true. But after failing often and sometimes quite painfully, I realized that I was taking failure entirely too personally. Yes, I understood that I must take responsibility for my actions. However, I had to make the distinction between failing at a task or goal and failing at being a decent person.

I realized that failure did not have to be linked to my identity as a person, but it certainly was linked to my ability to do certain tasks or accomplishing certain goals. I also had to come to the understanding that failing at something is nothing more than an opportunity to learn. When I failed at something, it didn't prove that I had no worth or value. It showed that I lacked skill, know-how, or competency in a particular area. Not that I was incapable of learning, but that there was some specific area I needed to improve. It was funny to me when I realized that failure helped to define my professional development plan.

I came to adopt a simple phrase, "If I fail, I need to focus." I now understand that failure is the key to my success. Failure is the flashlight that highlights an area where there is deficiency in my ability. Failure helps me to refine and identify potential areas of improvement. Failure is no longer my enemy, in fact it is my friend. In this book I would like to reintroduce you to my friend, Failure, and my other friend, Success. In these pages, I share my thoughts and experiences along my life journey and I encourage you to take a similar life journey of your own.

Chapter 2: Failure is not Disqualification

Have you ever attempted to accomplish a goal and failed miserably? A professional goal, a weight loss goal, or a goal to get a certain grade in a class? Do you remember what passed through your mind as you found out how far off the mark you were? If your experience was anything like mine, you probably had a series of emotions, thoughts, and feelings which were not at all pretty. It was more than likely worse if you had others depending on you and you failed -- now that's really difficult.

When you think about those times, what is your first response? Do you think about how difficult the task was or do you think about what must have been wrong with you that you failed? How you view the experience, even now sheds a lot of light on how you think about yourself today. Do you think about your specific actions that led to the failure? Or, do you think you failed because you are stupid, unskilled or incompetent?

Based on certain experiences, we may tend to beat up ourselves. Why do we tend to do that when we fail? I believe that a better solution is to evaluate ourselves in light of the intensity and complexity of the situation. Do you know that a challenge would not be a challenge if there was not the possibility of failing?

The Traditional View of Failure

Failure has been given an undo amount of attention! We traditionally think about failure as not achieving an assigned task to the specified level of accuracy or precision. This is very true. Many definitions of failure focus on the ability or inability to accomplish a task. Yet the definition does not tell us that a person is unable to learn from their failures. Nor does it tell us if a person will be able to bounce back to a high level of success. Despite this, we often remove people who fail from the headlines and usher them to the back of the line. It's as if failure has ruined them for life.

This view is evident in how we promote some, in how we include others, and in how we publicly recognize people. Think about it, if a person gets all F's, we tend to think that s/he is not smart or that there is something inherently wrong with them. We immediately start trying to find out what is broken in them. Rather we admit it or not, we start to wonder if they have some emotional, mental, or learning issue. Not only that, we think people who fail at the things that we value, are somehow inferior or deficient. They are broken and need to be fixed.

This view of failure often permeates everything. It is in the work environment, the school environment, and in society in general. In schools, if you fail a subject, it's not because the teacher couldn't teach or the content wasn't explained in a learning style that matched with yours. NO, it's all about you are not a good student. The sad part of all of this is that so many people have truly accepted such ideas about themselves. How many of us have been sidetracked and sidelined by thoughts of inferiority or incompetency due to our belief in the traditional view of failure? How many of us are sitting on the sidelines now instead of engaging in life toe-to-toe?

Disqualified by Choice

News flash! You can only be sidelined when you choose to be! That's right, just because someone tells me to get out of the game of life, doesn't mean I must do that. Can I give myself the benefit of the doubt? Others may have seen me fail, but they can also see me make a good comeback story, too! I learned about this important concept through *The Third Option*, an international skills-based marriage program. I participated in a small group and learned some "comeback" skills. This program developed something called the "Bill of Rights for Married Couples." But it works for everyone. The program highlights the rights that all human beings have, and among these it emphasizes that an individual should be given the benefit of the doubt when they mess up. Everyone is autonomous and should be treated as such, claiming their right to start over towards a path of success.

I have come to see that these rights are appropriate for all people as they communicate one major point. We all can choose to engage life on terms we agree to or we can choose to let other people set the agenda for us. One of my former mentors once told me," If you do not set your own agenda, someone else will set it for you." This is true as it relates to failure. We can choose to disqualify ourselves and follow the agenda that someone else has set for us, or we can choose to set a new agenda for ourselves, stay in the game and not be sidelined. The choice is yours. What will you do? Are you in or out?

Choose to Persist

I had the privilege of attending an awards event for my daughter at a college in Kentucky. During the event, the keynote speaker shared his story on how he graduated from the college. He shared that he grew up in a neighborhood in the urban core like many students. He did not fully buy into the whole college idea when he first left home. He was the child who "escaped" the rough environment by taking advantage of the opportunity to attend college. This may sound familiar to some of you. He struggled, not just with being at college but with if he could handle the responsibility of being in school. He entered college academically behind and he was angry about being unprepared. He was challenged by the pace and difficulty of the assignments so he acted out and caused a number of problems on campus. As a result, he was kicked out of college three times. Yet he persisted. Each time he got kicked out he harassed the school until they relented to allow him back in to complete his degree.

The lesson that I took away from his discussion is this: Persistence may not be easy, but it is productive. How do I know it was productive for this speaker? He felt he was not capable of learning, he had learning disabilities, and he had anger issues, but he also had a choice. He decided to focus on learning how to overcome his challenges. Instead of finding something broken in his character, he focused on his deficiencies in skills, ability, or competency and made a plan to compensate. He decided to persist and not sit on the sideline.

I can't emphasize it enough, he had to make a choice! You must make a choice as well. What will it be, sideline or finish line? By the way, the speaker is now a lawyer and a high-ranking member in his state's government. What a difference persistence can make!

Chapter 3: Lessons from the Valley

My mentor, let's just call him Coach, related a stirring account of the two games that he lost while coaching high school basketball. In the first example, he lost a championship game but won at the game of life. There was a player on his team, in fact, he was the best player on the squad, but he got into trouble off the court. He violated a major rule and forced Coach to make a major decision. Coach decided to bench him and did not let him play in the important game. Not only did he not let him play, he made him dress in street clothes. Coach wanted to make it clear so that everyone knew he was not playing in the game. Needless to say, they lost the game.

Coach relates a similar story in which a player made the choice to use illegal drugs. As a result, he had to bench the player and not allow him to play. In both instances, the players made choices that forced Coach to make decisions of his own. Coach often shares how difficult these decisions were to make. He also relates that when he looks back on these events, he could not imagine making different decisions. But it wasn't easy to make those decisions at the time.

There were two major events that occurred following these games. After the game in our first example, Coach was not so sure that he had made the right decision. He asked one of the other players about the choice to bench the "star" player. The young man's answer was profound. He basically stated that if Coach had allowed the guy to play in the game, Coach would have lost the respect of the other players and would have gone against what he stood for as a person. Wow! Coach failed at basketball but won at life. The points that were scored that day in the locker room after the game, were far more important than the points scored on the court during the game.

In the second example, Coach had to talk to the parents. He had to tell them that their son could not play. After the family left, the mother soon returned and let Coach know that the father had a major role in the failure of their son. The mother said that the family was forced to take assessment of their circumstances. Coach explained that years later the student thanked him for the decision to bench him. It taught him an important lesson about making right decisions and the high cost of consequences. Failure -- It does not always feel good but it can do some good.

But wait, not all experiences end in positive ways. If you were to ask Coach about the fallout for benching the child in the championship game, he will tell you that there was a cost. More than 15 years later, the father of the child still doesn't speak to him.

Coach showed me that failure doesn't take place in a vacuum. It happens right in the middle of life. One of my favorite quotes is, "Yea though I walk through the valley of the shadow of death, I will fear no evil..." Failure takes place in a shadowy valley. It may be painful and it may be embarrassing. One thing is for sure, you may not choose to enter a valley, but you can choose how you go through the valley. What valley of failure are you in now? What can you learn while there?

Pain can be Healthy

I don't like pain. I don't avoid pain, but I don't look for ways to experience it either. Take the dentist for example. I once met a young high school student who said she loved everything about the dentist office and that she could go every week. I kid you not. She likes the dentist so much that her future college plans include going to school to be a dentist. I wish her well.

This is not how I feel. I tolerate the dentist. I have had some work done that required the use of big needles. Let's say that I survived. Many of us would associate the dentist with pain. It is usually pain that draws us there, pain shows up while they are working, and pain usually stays for a little while after the visit. Yet all of this pain is necessary if we are to remain healthy. Fillings are needed to prevent additional pain and tooth loss. I won't go into details on how they do this, let's just say pain is healthy because it lets us know that something needs our attention.

How do pain and health relate in the context of failure? Let's look at Coach again. Do you think it was painful for the team to lose the championship game? Do you think it was painful for the family to have to face the reality of their problems? I would say yes. However, would you also say that this kind of pain is healthy? I'm not suggesting that we seek out pain. I am suggesting that we find positive lessons in the pain and failure that we have in our lives. I'm sure pain is there, because failure is there, somewhere. Find it. Face, it. Deal with it. Endure it. On the other side of the pain there can be a healthier you.

Embarrassment is Optional

Imagine this scene. You are at a major banquet with a few hundred people: leaders, coworkers, and your supervisor. You walk on stage to present an award recipient with their trophy. You reach to pick up the glass trophy, it slips from your hand and hits the stage with a loud thud. It doesn't break so you bend down pick it up, hand it to the recipient, shake their hand and exit stage left. As you get off stage you become aware of how crazy this is. You now have a choice to make. Will you melt away because of embarrassment or will you take it on the chin and chalk this up as a learning experience because you can't hide it, or run from it? Yes, this happened to me. I was a director of a department and this was our annual awards banquet.

Was this a failure on my part? Some would say yes, others would say no. I'm certain I lost some cool points but I also learned a valuable lesson. Up until that event took place, I was very particular about looking a certain way in public. I had learned to save face and tried very hard to be seen as a mature, have-it-all-together young man. I was a young director. I was one of the youngest ever at this organization and I wanted to project the right image.

There I was, at a crossroad of sorts. I could laugh or be embarrassed. I chose to laugh. I took a few barbs and jokes from people for a while but this eventually passed. This was a simple example of failing in the public eye where embarrassment is possible. I'm sure there are others who have far more painful and embarrassing situations of failure that come to mind.

Regardless of the situation, the choice is the same. Embarrassment or taking it on the chin? Your choice will take you down a specific path. One path forces you to cover up and protect yourself. The other forces you to open up and embrace a lighter side of failure. It is true that there are some things you can't change. There are no do-overs. You have what you have. The question is, "How do you make the best of a situation?"

I chose to find the humor in the situation, to recognize that I am not perfect, and to give myself permission to be human. I was fortunate that this situation wasn't too serious. I could have been reprimanded for embarrassing my boss. Fortunately, that did not happen. I only had a bruised ego and a few jokes made about things. Again, your situation may be more severe; however, you still have a choice about how you will respond. What will it be?

Standing is a Choice

Failure can take on many forms. Not all failures involve losing a ballgame, missing a sales target, or poor grades in school. Some of the larger challenges come with ethical and moral choices. It has been my experience that many failures come at the cost of personal principles.

I remember early in my teen years I found myself in a difficult situation. I was 14 years old, going into 9th grade and soon to be a father. I ran from that responsibility. I was scared and in a self-imposed emotional prison. I had violated my principles and I did not want to disappoint others by my actions, but that was no longer an option. Many people had one image of me and I believed that I violated their trust. I failed to honor the principles that I publicly espoused to be right and true. It was at that time that I felt stuck. I was ashamed and led a double life for many years. I had one public life and one private life. I almost lost myself between those two worlds. I experienced a similar situation at 19 years old. I failed myself again. My sons were not a mistake or a failure; I am proud of them. Yet, I do regret that they had to be negatively impacted by my bad choices as a teenage father.

I am not proud of that period of my life and there are many failures that I have had that are equally as painful. I am thankful however. The pain and the struggles of that period of life have helped to make me a better man. I have tasted the bitterness of longing: wanting to hold and love my sons, but being forbidden to do so because of immature games, broken relationships and life done out of order. What does this have to do with standing? I remember at the age of 21, I was challenged to stand and deliver more than just words. I was challenged to be what I was talking about, not just be a talker. I had to choose if I would stand and walk in a new direction or sit and waste away in my failures.

I chose to stand! I began the hard work of self-reflection and growth. I challenged my faith. If it was real, and my belief system was real, then it should be able to transform my life. I found out that this standing idea is a process that takes you on a journey. I have had a tremendous amount of pain and failure but I have also had an overwhelming amount of joy and success. I have learned important lessons in my standing process.

Gratefulness: I am grateful to have what I have. I still hurt because my relationships with my sons are nowhere near how I would like them to be. But they exist. Bravo! Not an editorial comment, but you made me cheer, nonetheless.

Humility in Remorse: I can't undo the pain I've caused. This leaves me with a dull ache for those I've hurt and the life I've wasted. I believe I am more empathetic as a result.

Redemption: I have been given the opportunity to have loving relationships with my wife and daughters. I must accept their love because it is easy for me to feel undeserving. I can make different decisions now.

The valley of failure was not gentle or kind to me. I have the marks and scars to prove this. However, the valley has been life altering. I am not the same person I used to be. I pray that as I journey through my future valleys that I am transformed even more. And think about it, it all started when I chose to stand--in the valley.

CHAPTER 4: Failure is Not Permanent

Have you failed at something and believe that you are not able to bounce back from the experience? If so, you are not alone. Failure has a way of convincing us that life is over just because we have failed. One of my favorite accounts that relates to this concept, involves a group of people that betrayed their leader. They were all scared and fearful for their lives yet the group agreed to stick together. When it came down to it, when it really mattered the most, when the leader needed the most support, the group was nowhere to be found. In fact, when questioned about the relationship, one of the stronger group members denied that he even knew the leader. How is that for "having someone's back"?

Things did not go well for the leader and the group was disbanded for a period of time. After a while, the leader came back looking for his group. The leader was especially interested in finding one of his closest friends who betrayed and denied him. His friend was so full of shame when the leader found him that he had a difficult time accepting his leader's greetings and concern. How else should he feel after failing so miserably? Instead of hammering on him and tearing him down, the leader forgave him and gave him added responsibility. In fact he took on a central leadership role after the leader left.

This story is a great example of how failure does not have to be permanent. Although the guy failed, he could accept the hand up from his leader and became one of the strongest leaders of the group. Can you find yourself in this story? Maybe, maybe not. However, you might know someone who needs to know that failure is not permanent. Pass this idea along. You never know who might need it

You Can Only Fail if You Try

Hanging in my living room is a framed quote from Confucius that goes something like this," Our greatest glory is not in never failing but in getting up every time that we do." If there is one thing that I have learned about life, it is that life is not easy. You have probably figured that out by now as well.

I'm reminded of a young man who I have grown to admire and respect. While talking one day, he recounted his life story. He was raised by a mother who was on drugs and by a father who was sometimes there and other times not. By the age of twelve he was in the foster care system. By the age of sixteen he was homeless. He moved thousands of miles away from his hometown to attend Job Corps in the Midwest. This is where I met him.

He was interested in attending college and he needed someone to help him transition into higher education, which is why he sat across the desk from me. We worked together to resolve his issues and he succeeded in enrolling in college, continuing his academic journey. He had difficulty choosing between a few majors but finally settled on a path that led to his associate degree. I remember feeling very proud of him as he walked across the stage to receive his diploma.

His journey to the stage was not easy. He had failed several times along the way. First, he had been removed from the Job Corps program because he had been hanging around with the wrong crowd. However, he did complete his GED before leaving Job Corps. Also, he had a few run-ins with certain staff at the college but he sought council from a few trusted adults and was able to work out each problem. He persisted until graduation. It wasn't easy but he made it.

At the time that I am writing this book, he has now graduated from a four-year college and is working to complete his graduate degree. Along the way he faced even more failures that threatened his success. As I watched him struggle through his process I was reminded that he failed, not because he was incompetent, but because he tried to achieve a dream.

Failure can only be failure if you, like my friend, are attempting to try something that causes you to reach beyond your current reality. What are you reaching for? What failures have caused you to think about quitting?

Are you courageous enough to try again? I encourage you to try again. As the nursery rhyme says,

> "Here's a lesson you should heed, Try, Try again.
> If at first you don't succeed, Try, Try again.
> Then your courage should appear,
> For if you will persevere,
> You will conquer; never fear, Try, Try again"

Each Attempt Teaches Something New

Thomas Edison was attributed to have said that he did not fail 10,000 times, he just found 10,000 ways that did not work. Now that is something! What can you learn from failing 10,000 times? I would say that you can learn a lot about yourself. I am reminded of an anonymous poem I learned as a child entitled "I Search". It goes;

> I search myself,
> To find myself,
> Inside my self
> To know who I am
> And why I am who I am
> I search.

Failure has a way of forcing us to make hard decisions and search for answers. It causes us to look within to determine what we will do. Often, at the point of failure, we must decide to give in or give it our all. We must decide to accept responsibility and not to blame something or someone else for our situation. I believe that one of the hardest decisions that we can make is the decision to be honest with ourselves about our role in our failure.

When talking to my young friend who is pursuing his graduate degree, I was struck by his willingness to admit his role in the problems and failures that he has had. He took responsibility. Unlike my friend, I have been known to run from my responsibility. This tendency to protect myself has some good qualities; like keeping me from danger and helping me not to rush into some situations. On the other hand, this tendency has had some negative consequences as well.

I believe that I've avoided responsibility in the past because of my bent towards self-preservation. This bent includes shrinking back from certain challenges because of the possibility of failing. I must admit that failure has taught me that things don't get easier when you run from them.

Failure is a good teacher but a hard task-master. If one is willing to listen and pay attention, failure can teach you quite a bit. Below is a list of a few things that I have learned from failure:

- Falling down is painful, getting up is tedious, and going forward is rewarding.

- Failure is only an option when it is permitted to be one.

- Failure hurts but I can eventually get over it.

- Having a sense of adventure helps to put failure in perspective.

- Having faith helps to make failure a stepping stone.

What has failure taught you? If you say nothing, think again. It may have taught you to play it safe or to criticize yourself and others. Or, it may have taught you to dig deeper and fight harder. One thing is for sure, you do not fail without learning something new with each attempt at success. I encourage you to stop and think about what failure is trying to teach you. You might be surprised by the lessons that are waiting for you.

"10,000 attempts. 10,000 failures. 10,000 lessons learned." Thomas Edison succeeded on the 10,001 attempts. Failure is not permanent unless you stop trying. As the failed leader and my friend learned, it is easy to get sidelined by failure but you must choose to stay in the game. You never know when your opportunities for success will come. Success comes to those who keep trying. I'll end this chapter with another thought from Thomas Edison, "Many of life's failures are men who did not realize how close they were to success when they gave up." Don't give up, success may be right around the corner. Failure isn't permanent.

Chapter 5: Stuck Along the Journey

Many years ago while commuting to work, I had a flat tire on I-75, a major highway that runs between Dayton and Cincinnati, Ohio. It was rainy, cold, and cars were rushing past me not more than 5 feet away. I was miserable while I was trying to change my tire. I could get it done but in the process, I got soaked, endured the heart-racing experience of a semi-truck zooming past, and I had to nurse a few bruised knuckles. All of this happened while I was on my journey from home to work. I was sidelined for about an hour or so and ended up being late to work.

This experience is not unlike experiences that many of you are having along the journey of life. You were moving from a place of hope to a place of opportunity in your life. You had goals and dreams. You started with an end in mind and now you find yourself sidelined along the journey. You may find yourself soaked with discouragement, bruised by impatience, and held hostage by fear. Whatever your situation, I want to encourage you to keep changing the tire. Focus on fixing the problem that may be hindering you and stay committed to finishing what you started. Don't give up just because you've experienced a flat along the way. You can re-tool, re-think, and re-engage in your dream. Will you?

Bogged Down in Discouragement

If anyone tells you that they have not experienced the heaviness of discouragement, I would seriously doubt if they are being honest. Everyone faces seasons of time along the journey when they must decide if they have the courage to continue moving forward. This wrestling match is not a sign of weakness or of your inability to succeed. It is a pit stop along the way that allows you to examine the content of your true character or what you are really made of, so to speak..

The word "discourage" literally means to take away courage. Courage can be taken away in a variety of ways. If you are in a situation that requires more from you than you think you can give, you can become "discouraged". If you have attempted something time and time again and have failed over and over again, you can be "dis-couraged". If you are riddled with guilt because of all the things you wished you would have done differently, you could be "dis-couraged". What happens when courage is taken away? You focus on the problem instead of the solution. You recite all the reasons why you cannot go forward. You waste time doing things that look productive but really aren't. You may even sabotage your success by dragging your feet so that you give someone the excuse to not promote, hire, or support you. If you are discouraged you may feel depressed or overcome with sorrow.

Discouragement can feel like walking with concrete blocks on your feet or carrying a heavy load while walking up stairs. You may feel drained and overwhelmed. Just like I was soaked to the bone by the rain on the side of the road, you may be soaked to the bone by discouragement. If this is where you find yourself today, I want to offer you this acronym of truth that I have recently adopted regarding hope. I invite you to remember this acronym:

Having

Obstinate

Persistence, in-spite of

Everything

Hope requires that you persist until you see the reality of what you are hoping for. This requires that you focus on where you are going, not where you are now or where you have come from. Hope requires you to see what others may not see. Sometimes you may be the only one who believes in your ability to achieve and succeed. Even if this is true, you must choose to persist until the end.

Persisting to the end reminds me of an old Jewish saying, "Forgetting those things which are behind, I press towards the prize of the high calling...." Since I am a firm believer that each of us has purpose, I believe that I have an obligation to keep going until I see my purpose fulfilled. However, along the way, discouragement may act like a secret agent who has been assigned to distract you from your purpose. This agent's greatest weapons are our emotions and feelings regarding the failures of the past. We all have failures. After we have learned from them, then we must turn away from them and press towards the future that is calling us. Can you hear your future calling you? It's a high calling. It might be in a high frequency so you may have to listen in ways you have never done before. You must press through your discouragement and move towards the higher calling. No one can press for you. You must decide to get up, lean forward, and press against discouragement

Think about this. If you can be "dis-couraged", you can be "en-couraged." It's an amazing thing. With each step you take towards your goal, you find that courage begins to re-enter. You find yourself becoming "en-couraged" as you make progress towards your future goal. Today is the first day of the rest of your life, what will you do with it? It begins with one step. Step into your future inspite of the difficulty that you find yourself in today. Remember the words of Albert Einstein," In the middle of difficulty lies opportunity." If you are in difficulty today, do everything you can to find the opportunity in the middle of your current situation. This will help lead you to your tomorrow.

Intimidated by Fear

Fear and discouragement are partners. You often find them running in the same circles. In my life, I have often found that if one is present in my circumstances, the other is not far behind. Fear often holds you down while discouragement beats you up. They seem to be the enforcers trying to keep you huddled on the side of the road.

You may have heard the following acronym for the word Fear --False Evidence Appearing Real. Fear is powered by the unknown. I remember growing up and being afraid to fight a kid in the neighborhood. I avoided his house around the corner because I though he was tougher than me. I avoided him for a few weeks and then I realized I had to do something. I walked past his house and he came out to fight me. We stood there facing each other with our hands up. He hit me and I hit him as hard as I could. He backed away talking a lot but not coming back at me. I turned and walked away. I never had a problem with him again after that.

Fear wanted me to believe a lie. The lie was that the other guy would hurt me, or that I would run and not stand my ground. Fear played with my doubts about myself. It tried to make me think the other guy was bigger and stronger than he really was. The reality was that we both were afraid. The reality was the other guy didn't hit as hard as I imagined him to hit. The reality was that I hit him hard enough for him to back away from me for good. The reality was different from the "evidence" that fear presented to me.

This is how fear operates. It holds you down by allowing you to create a false picture about your current or future state. It starts with a grain of truth, like this guy could hurt me, and then allows you to fill in the blanks with a negative imagination, like I'll look stupid to everyone in the neighborhood when he beats me up. It truly is false evidence appearing real. Now I'm not suggesting you engage in physical altercations, but you get my point here. If you let fear linger long enough, it will beat you into a mindset of failure.

When you fail, you may feel discouraged and you may fear trying again. Along the journey, fear can sideline you with intimidation while discouragement can weigh you down and sap your strength. These two may often tag team against you. If you find yourself in a fight with these two, don't listen to fear and don't get distracted by discouragement. Focus on your future, fight until you win, and finish what you started.

Chapter 6: From Lessons to Principles

I had the pleasure of attending a workshop conducted by Dr. Adolph Brown. Dr. Brown is a national and international motivational speaker and master teacher. His presentations are engaging and challenging from start to finish. In his workshops, you find yourself wondering, "How can I rise to the challenge of setting higher personal standards and expectations?"

In his presentation he states, "I am not better than anyone else, I have just messed up more than others. This has given me the opportunity to share the lessons that I have learned from those failures and events." As he shared about his life story, a young man from an under-resourced community, raised by a caring mother and a strong grandfather; I realized that he discovered that power of "the lesson learned."

The Power of the Lesson Learned

I have failed and struggled and I anticipate that failure will not be so kind as to let me graduate from its school. I'm ok with that because failure is not my end. The challenge that faces many is not will we fail, but "how" will we fail. Will we fail into defeat or will we fail into success? We can be like the mythical animal, the Phoenix, and rise from the ashes of our failures.

As previously stated, along life's journey you will fail. Failure is a companion of anyone who persists into success. Again, the question is not will you fail, but what will you learn from your failure? Some lessons are easy to learn. Some require time, while others require more from you than you think you can give. I once heard someone say that experience is a hard teacher. It gives you the test first, then it gives you the lesson. Failure must have learned a lot from experience. Have you learned from your failure? Not everyone can answer yes to this question. I have learned a few things. The power of the lesson learned is that lessons can be distilled into principles to guide your life. Allow me to share the "Life Principles" that failure has taught me.

Life Principle # 1:"It doesn't matter what color the hand is that is holding the knife in my back. Surround yourself with good people."

People will betray you and use you. Failure has taught me that life can be a lonely journey. Life is hard. There are any number of challenges (i.e. failing grades, jobs been downsized, broken personal relationships, addictions, etc.) that can sidetrack and sideline you along the journey. Failure is inevitable. How you manage it and overcome it is up for discussion. It's not always easy to determine who to trust as you travel this road. However, you must trust someone. Finding good people to experience this journey with is essential to your spiritual, emotional, and physical health. Here are some pointers taken from Life Principle # 1:

- Just because a person looks like you, has a similar background as yours, and comes from similar economic situations, it doesn't mean that they are a fit for your journey.

- Character trumps charisma every time. Make sure to surround yourself with people who won't compromise the truth or cut corners.

- Beware of the person who is more concerned about your feelings than they are for what is right.

- Make sure a person is walking with you because you share the same passion. Passion outlasts a good idea when things get tough.

- Be willing to be lonely. Know yourself well enough to care for your own self so you are not desperate to be accepted.

We live in a world that values the superficial. We have created artificial barriers and have ignored the real barriers that stop our successes. This is a failure in itself. You may have to deal with your fear of unknown people and cultures to achieve a high level of success. Don't manufacture your own failure because you discount people who could very well enrich and enliven your life.

Life Principle # 2: "People will make you a king and then crucify you. Leadership is lonely but necessary."

This principle has been an underpinning to my leadership philosophy. I have painfully come to realize that you will have more people who talk about change than are willing to undergo the hard transformation that change requires. Since people have a low tolerance for pain when things get difficult in a change process, they look for someone to blame for the pain. When this occurs, here are a few pointers while managing people through the painful process of change.

Here are pointers from principle 2:

- Create an urgent future story for your group or organization. Everyone must be able to see where they are going and why it is important to get there.

- Give them clear indicators of success, consistent feedback, clear consequences and involve them in setting the direction.

- Put the focus on the work, not on you. Create a plan that assesses where you are, where you need to go, and how you will get there. People should be motivated by the work and the purpose of the work not by your personality.

- Learn the strengths and weaknesses of your direct reports and position them for success.

- Resource them, empower them, and support them. Fight the fights they are not able to fight and let them fight the fights that require them to grow.

- You must grow and be honest in recognizing that you have weaknesses.

- Celebrate often and celebrate well.

- Beware of the flattery that you may receive. Never believe the news clippings about yourself, or "drink" the Kool-aid. You are never as good as you think you are. Don't worry, you are never as bad as you think you are either.

It is important to realize that there is always someone who can do what you do. They may or may not do it better, but more than likely they can get the job done. Do your best anyway. Advance the vision of the organization and leave the place better than when you arrived.

Life Principle # 3: "I am one decision away from destroying everything that I value. Therefore, I value my values."

Life is very unforgiving. There is a myth that our society likes to give people second chances and that you will be restored back to the place from which you fell. This is only a myth. Mistakes can cost you everything. A decision that was intentional can cost everything plus your future. Dr. Adolph Brown speaks of the difference between a mistake and a bad decision. The main difference is if you thought about it before you did it, it wasn't a mistake. We make bad decisions and then want to cover them over with a cloak of innocence.

This was a hard lesson for me. I had lived a portion of my life making excuses for my bad decisions. I had to learn that the damage you do to yourself and others cannot be excused away. Sometimes, "I'm sorry" is not good enough. There are times in life where there are no "do-overs" and you must live with the consequences of the decisions that you make. Failure has taught me the following points about Life Principle # 3:

- Work to deal with your shortcomings. We all have faults but somethings left unattended can grow out of control.

- Understand the value of what you have. Don't take things for granted.

- You are as sick as your secrets. Some of our failures are due to the things that we keep hidden. Seek help so that you can be healthy.

- Value your values. We make decisions based on what we believe and value. If your decisions contradict your values you might want to question whether you value your values.

- Be willing to correct and heal broken relationships and friendships. The emotional pressure of the past can encourage bad decisions for the future.

- Set boundaries. Learn to set boundaries. Don't carry someone else's monkey on your back. There is power in saying no.

The funny thing about consequences is that they don't care about your intentions. Consequences react to what you do, not what you meant to do. Consequences are "amoral" and are unconcerned about whether something is right or wrong. So, be careful with your decisions for they are like bullets from a gun. Once the gun is fired, you cannot put the bullet back in the barrel, nor can you control what damage it will do.

If you are willing to heed the lessons that failure can teach, you are moving down the road to success. We all can grow from the past when we gain principles and knowledge from the lessons of the past.

Appendix A: Implement a P.L.A.N

Using the Lessons Learned

In chapter four we discussed preparing a plan to re-engage areas where we have failed. In the educational research literature, this process would be designed to help increase self-efficacy. Self-Efficacy is the belief in one's ability to advocate and perform tasks independent of assistance and help which leads to the accomplishment of goals. Below are tips and a simple acronym to help with the process of developing a plan that can lead to greater self-efficacy.

Prepare: Before you get back into the game you need to make sure that you have done the internal work of identifying what lessons you have learned. If you do not identify the lessons, you cannot determine what you need to learn. Make a list of the internal and external factors that contributed to the failure. Did you lack sufficient knowledge or skill? Did you lack self-control or have poor time management skills? Did you have an addiction? There could be any number of issues.

Learn: Seek the help you need to address these issues. Grow in proficiency in these areas.

Attempt: Practice, practice, practice! Find volunteer opportunities or other opportunities to put what you have learned in to practice. Take small steps initially until you become comfortable with your new ability. Achieve small success at implementing the new skills.

Negotiate: This is where the most challenging work takes place. You have to negotiate environments where you failed previously. You must confront the "failure tapes" that may be playing in your head. You may enter environments that generate strong emotional responses. This is where the stages of "learn and attempt" will be so helpful. You will need to remind yourself that you are not the same person that you were during the initial challenges. You have learned new things, dealt with the challenges of yesterday, and have gained new competencies.

Appendix B: My Success Creed

Dr. Michael and Jill Gaines

With every experience, with every choice,
on every day, with every step on my Journey of
Success:

I choose to answer my purpose.
I choose to face my fears.
I choose to challenge myself.
I choose to face my failures.

When I fail, And I will fail,
I commit to seek help from others.
I commit to learn from constructive criticism.
I commit to stay off the sidelines of life.
I will learn from my failures.

Failure is not my destination.
Failure is not my name.
Failure is not who I am.
Failure is merely an act!

I am gifted.
I am talented.
I am capable.
I am a success.

I am not a failure who happened to succeed!
I am a success who learns through failure!
I will learn to
Fail Into Success!

www.ingramcontent.com/pod-product-compliance
Lightning Source LLC
Chambersburg PA
CBHW071327200326
41520CB00013B/2885